START SMALL, THINK BIG

small, sparkling
Raindrop

by
Mary Auld

illustrations by
Lou Baker Smith

consultant
Dr Nicholas Souter, Conservation International

I am a small, sparkling raindrop – the first to fall from my cloud. I am made of water. Thousands of other raindrops will fall with me. Together, we are rain.

Water is a clear liquid. In small quantities, it forms a drop.

Rainwater is fresh and clean.

Raindrops form in clouds. When they get big and heavy enough, they fall to the ground.

Here is where I land on the Earth.
My weight starts me rolling downwards.
It is the start of my journey to the sea.

Animals drink some raindrops.

Some raindrops soak into the ground, helping plants to grow.

Some raindrops pool together to form puddles.

I join with other raindrops as I roll downhill. I get bigger and heavier.

Look! I have rolled into a stream. I race down the mountainside, splashing around rocks and tumbling over waterfalls.

As water rolls downhill, it comes together into streams. The running water wears away (erodes) the land, creating gullies and rocky banks.

Some rocks wear away faster than others. The water flows around them.

Waterfalls form when the stream erodes softer rock back to a ridge of hard rock. The water falls over it.

More streams join mine to make a river. It flows through a wet and steamy rainforest.

These mountains are in a tropical region. Lots of rain falls and it is hot. Thick rainforest grows in this steamy habitat.

Plants grow quickly here. Mosses and ferns grow right on the edge of the water.

Animals like it here because there is plenty to eat and drink.

Here is the Mekong, one of Earth's great rivers.
My smaller river runs into it. I mix with water drops from many other hills and mountains.

Along much of the Mekong, there are two seasons – one dry and one wet. The river floods after the heavy rains of the wet season.

My river is powerful. Its water carves out its valley and channels, on its journey to the ocean.

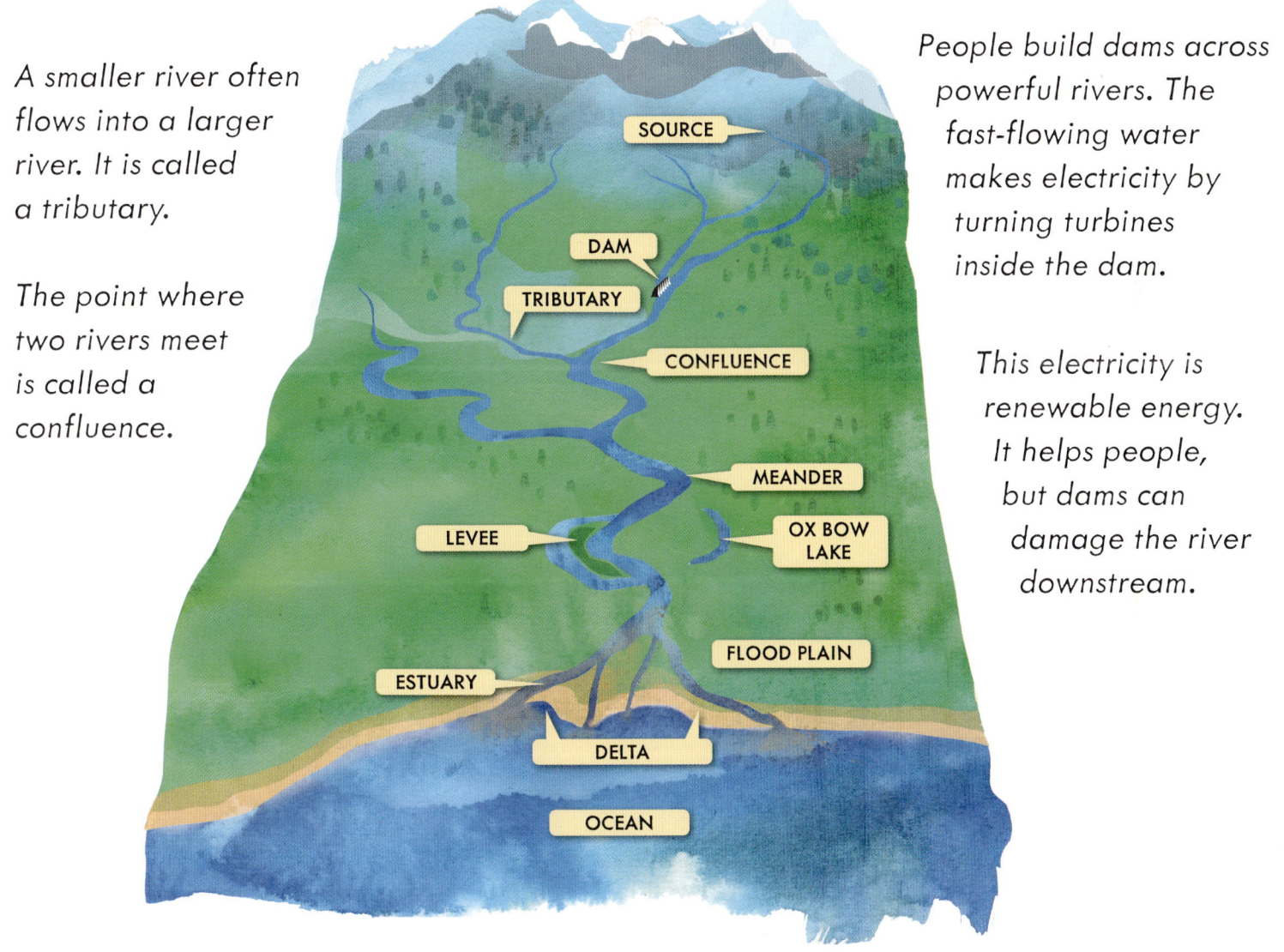

A smaller river often flows into a larger river. It is called a tributary.

The point where two rivers meet is called a confluence.

People build dams across powerful rivers. The fast-flowing water makes electricity by turning turbines inside the dam.

This electricity is renewable energy. It helps people, but dams can damage the river downstream.

A river delta is named after delta, a letter from the Greek alphabet, written like this: Δ. On a map, the river's channels form a delta shape.

Here is my river flowing slowly over a wide, flat valley.
It is huge now – over a kilometre wide. It has great bends and even islands.

When a river reaches flatter ground, it slows down and spreads out.

The water carries lots of sandy silt. Where the river flows very slowly, the silt drops from the water. Over time, this makes large bends and islands.

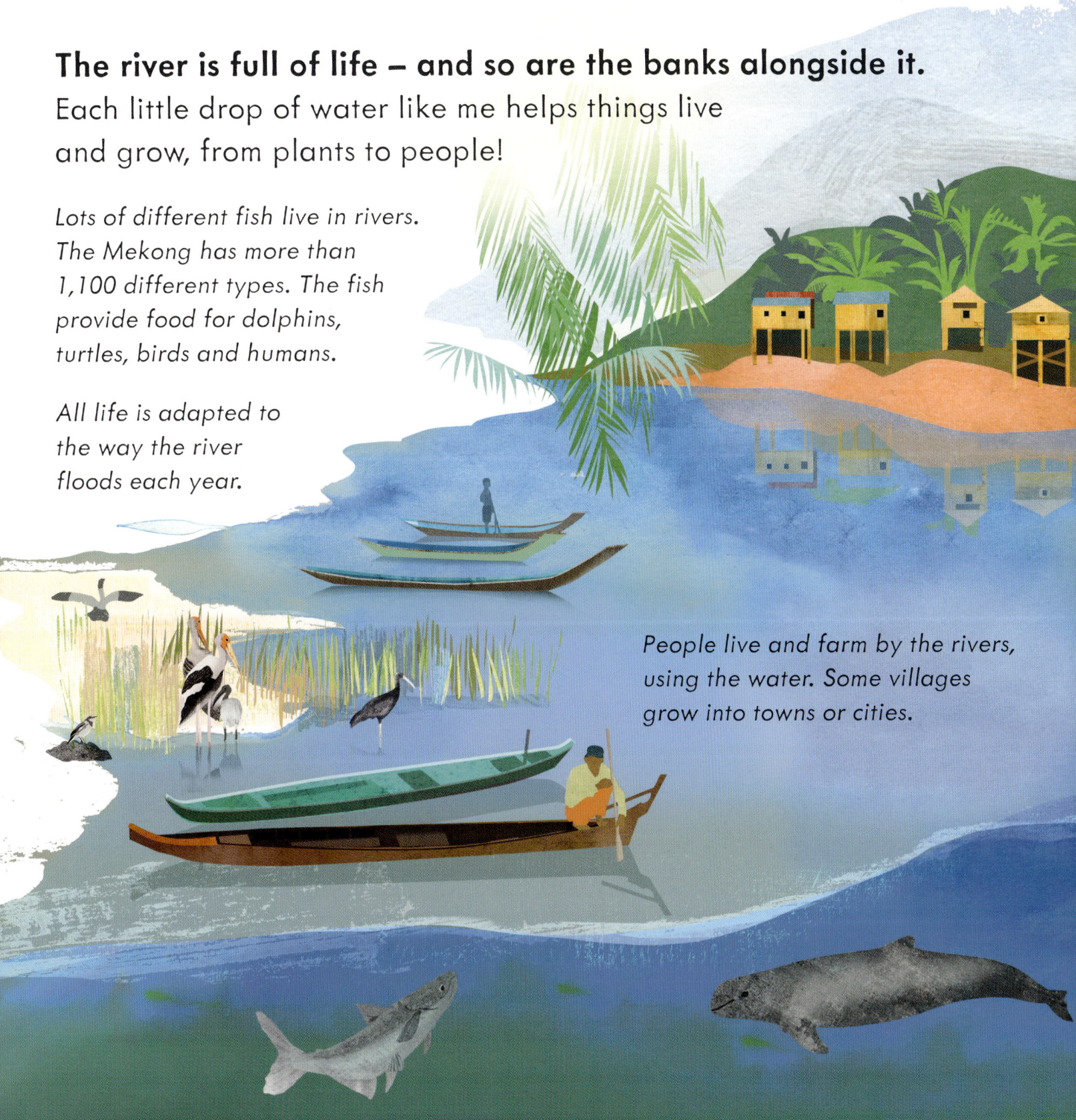

The river is full of life – and so are the banks alongside it.
Each little drop of water like me helps things live and grow, from plants to people!

Lots of different fish live in rivers. The Mekong has more than 1,100 different types. The fish provide food for dolphins, turtles, birds and humans.

All life is adapted to the way the river floods each year.

People live and farm by the rivers, using the water. Some villages grow into towns or cities.

Look at me now! I am one of billions of raindrops flowing through the Mekong delta.
I am nearing the sea.

Crops grow well in the rich and fertile soil. Farmers grow rice in flooded paddy fields.

As some rivers reach the sea, they drop more silt and form more islands. The river branches out around these to form a delta.

Here is a floating market. The farmers of the delta come here to sell their rice and other crops to the city people.

People grow so much rice in the Mekong delta it is known as 'the rice bowl' of southeast Asia.

The delta land often floods with the seasonal rains, so many homes are built on stilts to allow for this.

Climate change threatens delta areas. Rising sea levels could flood low-lying delta lands for ever.

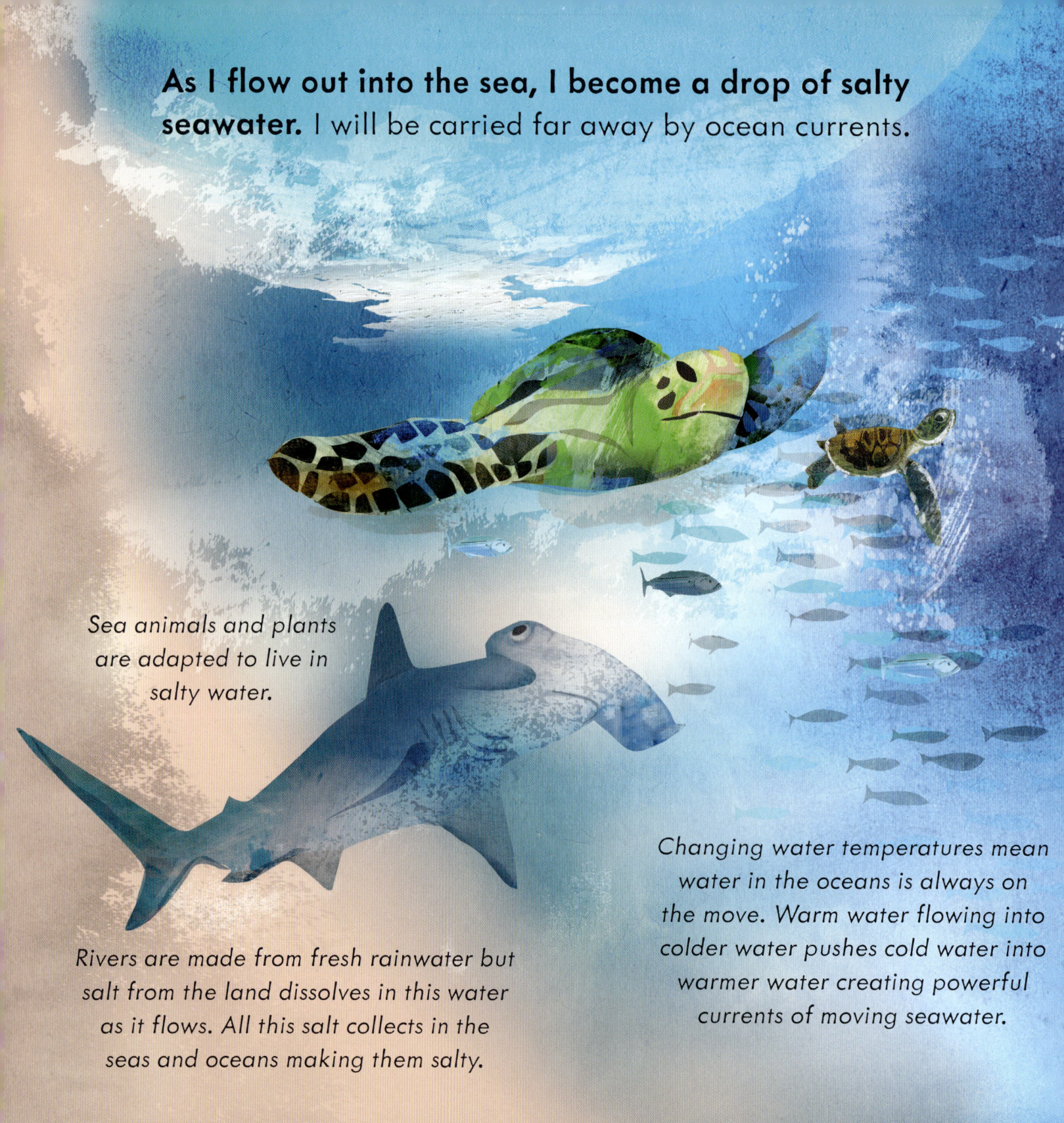

As I flow out into the sea, I become a drop of salty seawater. I will be carried far away by ocean currents.

Sea animals and plants are adapted to live in salty water.

Rivers are made from fresh rainwater but salt from the land dissolves in this water as it flows. All this salt collects in the seas and oceans making them salty.

Changing water temperatures mean water in the oceans is always on the move. Warm water flowing into colder water pushes cold water into warmer water creating powerful currents of moving seawater.

I have travelled nearly 2,000 km from where I fell in the Annamite Mountains to the South China Sea.

The Mekong is the twelfth longest river in the world. It starts in the Himalayas, the highest mountain range in the world.

The Mekong flows through six countries on its way to the sea, a journey of over 4,300 km. In China it is called Lancang.

Some rivers from the rainforests of the Annamite mountains run into the Mekong.

**Here is the wind blowing across the sea.
Look at the sails of the boats full of air.**

The blanket of air that surrounds Earth is called its atmosphere.

Changing temperatures cause air to move around Earth, just like water moves around the oceans.

Moving air makes the wind. It can be gentle or strong.

The sun shines down and I change again. This time I become water vapour. You cannot see me. I become part of the air.

Water moves around Earth in the air as well as in rivers and the sea. It changes, or evaporates, from a liquid to a gas called water vapour.

The way water moves and changes all the time helps make our weather.

Water can evaporate just about anywhere, but it happens faster when there is wind, warmth and a big area of water (like the ocean).

I have changed again. Look inside this cloud.
I am an ice crystal now!

Cirrus
high and wispy

7,000 metres

Air has water vapour in it, but it also has tiny specks of dust.

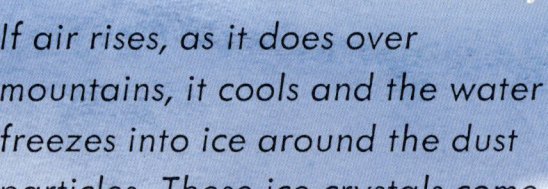

If air rises, as it does over mountains, it cools and the water freezes into ice around the dust particles. These ice crystals come together to form clouds.

Altostratus
mid-level, thin blanket

2,000 metres

Some clouds form high up in the atmosphere, others lower down.

Cumulonimbus
huge storm clouds

Cumulus
low and fluffy

Stratocumulus
low, flat and fluffy

Cirrocumulus
high and patterned

There are different types of cloud.
When the wind moves us around, we change shape and join together.

Ice crystals connect and get bigger, too. If they get heavy enough, they fall to the ground as precipitation — the name we give to water that falls from clouds.

Altocumulus
mid-level, broken and fluffy

Stratus
low and flat

Nimbostratus
low, dark and steady rain

I am about to fall, but will it be as rain, hail, sleet or snow?

SNOW
Ice crystals connect to form snowflakes. If it is cold, they fall as snow.

RAIN
When it is warmer, they melt as they fall to form rain.

SLEET
Sleet falls when snowflakes melt close to the ground.

HAIL
Falling rain may be blown back up high again. It freezes into balls of ice and falls to the ground as hail.

Here I am a fresh, sparkling raindrop again.
I am falling far away from where I fell before.
I bring life-giving water to another place on Earth.

Water may travel great distances through the atmosphere as vapour and in clouds.

Water that evaporates from the Pacific Ocean may eventually fall as rain over Africa.